Classifying Reptiles

LOUISE AND RICHARD SPILSBURY

Heinemann Library
Chicago, Illinois

Originated by Dot Gradations
Printed in Hong Kong, China by Wing King Tong

07 06 05 04 03
10 9 8 7 6 5 4 3 2 1

Library of Congress Cataloging-in-Publication Data
Spilsbury, Louise.
    Classifying reptiles / Louise and Richard Spilsbury.
        p. cm. -- (Classifying living things)
Summary: Explains what reptiles are and how they differ from other
animals, offering an overview of the life cycle of a variety of
reptiles, including snakes, turtles, lizards, and crocodiles.
Includes bibliographical references (p.   ) and index.
    ISBN 1-4034-0848-3 (lib. bdg. : hardcover) -- ISBN 1-4034-3348-8
(pbk.)
    1. Reptiles--Classification--Juvenile literature. 2.
Reptiles--Juvenile literature. [1. Reptiles.] I. Spilsbury, Richard,
1963- II. Title. III. Series.
    QL645 .S65 2003
    597.9--dc21

                                    2002015399

Acknowledgments
The publishers would like to thank the following for permission to reproduce photographs:
p. 4 NHPA/Daniel Zupanc; p. 5 Bruce Coleman/Joe McDonald; pp. 6, 21 Oxford Scientific Films;
p. 8 NHPA/Lady Philippa Scott; p. 9 NHPA/James Carmichael Jr.; p. 10 Oxford Scientific Films/
Tui De Roy; p. 11 Oxford Scientific Films/Philippe Henry; p. 12 Oxford Scientific Films/George
Bryce; p. 13 Bruce Coleman/MPL Fogden; p. 14 NHPA/A.N.T.; p. 15 NHPA/Stephen Dalton; p.
16 Bruce Coleman/John Cancalosi; p. 17 Oxford Scientific Films/Brian Kennedy; p. 18 Bruce
Coleman/Kim Taylor; p. 19 NHPA/Norbert Wu; p. 20 Bruce Coleman/Jane Burton; p. 22 Oxford
Scientific Films/Godfrey Merlen; p. 23 Bruce Coleman/Jim Watt; p. 24 Corbis/Peter Johnson; p.
25 NHPA/Daniel Heuclin; p. 26 Nature Picture Library; p. 27 NHPA/Eric Soder; p. 28 Oxford
Scientific Films/Michael Fogden; p. 29 Bruce Coleman/Alain Compost.

Cover photograph of Eyelash Viper babies reproduced with permission of Oxford Scientific
Films.

For Harriet and Miles, slow-worm enthusiasts.

Every effort has been made to contact copyright holders of any material reproduced in this
book. Any omissions will be rectified in subsequent printings if notice is given to the publishers.

Some words are shown in bold, **like this.** You can find out
what they mean by looking in the glossary.

Contents

How Classification Works

The earth is populated with an immense variety of living things—from the largest whale to the tiniest insect. Scientists believe that all these organisms are the **descendants** of a single group of very simple organisms that lived millions of years ago.

Classification can help us to understand how different organisms might be related to each other. It also helps us make better sense of the great variety of organisms, by sorting them into groups.

The body of a crocodile is one typical reptile shape. Other reptile groups such as snakes or turtles have different shapes.

Sorting life

Different living things are grouped according to the characteristics, or features, that they have in common. Some of these are obvious at first glance. For example, any animal you see with feathers is a bird. There are many features that are not so obvious, however. Fish, **mammals,** reptiles, birds, and **amphibians** are classified together because they are all **vertebrates.** Other less obvious characteristics used to classify organisms include how they **reproduce,** how they breathe, and the type of skin they have.

There are many different ways to classify, and scientists often disagree about the best way. Nevertheless, over time scientists have come up with a way of sorting all organisms.

From kingdoms to species

Living things are divided into huge groups called kingdoms. Plants, for example, are all grouped in one kingdom, and all animals are grouped in another. Each kingdom is made up of smaller groups, each called a **phylum**. A phylum contains several **classes**, classes contain **orders**, orders contain **families**, families contain **genera**, and genera contain **species**. A species is a single kind of organism, such as a tree iguana.

Common and scientific names

Many living things have a common name. These names are not always exact, and they can be different in different languages. For instance, there are two similar-looking types of iguanas that live on the Galapagos Islands. One feeds on land plants and the other on seaweed.

To distinguish between similar organisms, scientists give every species a two-part name. The first name is that of the genus the organism belongs to, and the second is the name of the species. The two types of Galapagos iguana are often called just "iguanas," but they belong to different species and have different scientific names. The land iguana has the name *Conolophus subcristatus* and the marine iguana is *Amblyrhynchus cristatus*.

iguana	Species
Iguana	Genus
Iguanas (Iguanidae)	Family
Lizards, snakes and worm lizards (Squamata)	Order
Reptiles (Reptilia)	Class
Chordates (Vertebrates)	Phylum
Animals (Animalia)	Kingdom

This pyramid shows the full classification for the common tree iguana—Iguana iguana.

What Is a Reptile?

Reptiles come in many shapes, sizes, and colors, from giant armored crocodiles and tortoises to brightly colored lizards and snakes. No matter how different reptiles look, they all share a number of characteristics that distinguish them from other types of animals:

- They are **vertebrates.**
- Their skin is covered by hard, protective **scales.**
- They **reproduce** using eggs, which they lay on land.
- They breathe oxygen using lungs.
- They are **cold-blooded**. They cannot control their own body temperature, so their bodies are always as hot or as cold as their surroundings.

Types of reptiles

Reptiles are classified by their body structure—both inside and out. The main reptile groups are lizards, snakes, turtles, and crocodiles. Lizards usually have four limbs, long bodies, and tails. Snakes always have no limbs. Turtles and tortoises have bony shells that cover their backs. Crocodiles look like lizards, but they have long, toothed jaws and heavily armored skin.

There are two other groups of reptiles. The first contains only two **species,** the tuataras, which look like lizards. Members of the other group, the amphisbaenids or worm lizards, look like snakes. These groups are classified separately because they have different skeletons than other reptiles have.

When we look at a snake's skeleton, the backbone can be seen clearly.

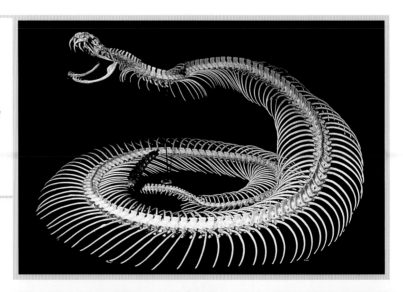

This table shows the **orders** of reptiles and gives some examples of main families and species.

Order	Suborder	Families	No. of species	Examples
Squamata (lizards, snakes, and amphisbaenids)	Lizards (Sauria)	Agamids (Agamidae)	300	Frilled dragon
		Anguids (Anguidae)	75	Slow-worm
		Beaded lizards (Helodermatidae)	2	Gila monster
		Chameleons (Chamaeleontidae)	85	Jackson's chameleon
		Geckos (Gekkonidae)	800	Leopard gecko
		Iguanas (Iguanidae)	650	Green iguana
		Lacertids (Lacertidae)	200	Viviparous lizard
		Monitors (Varanidae)	31	Komodo dragon
		Skinks (Scincidae)	1275	Blue-tailed skink
	Snakes (Serpentes)	Boas and pythons (Boidae)	60	Anaconda, tree python
		Rear-fangs (Colubridae)	1500	Garter snake
		Cobras (Elapidae)	170	Indian cobra
		Sea snakes (Hydrophiidae)	50	Dusky sea snake
		Blind snakes (Typhlopidae)	200	Southern blind snake
		Vipers (Viperidae)	180	Diamondback rattlesnake
Rynchocephalia (tuatara)		(Sphenodontidae)	2	Northern tuatara
Crocodilia (crocodiles, alligators, and caimans)		Alligators and caimans (Alligatoridae)	8	American alligator
		Crocodiles (Crocodylidae)	14	Nile crocodile
		Gavial (Gavialidae)	1	Gharial
Chelonia (reptiles with shells)	Turtles, tortoises, and terrapins (Cryptodira)	Marine turtles (Cheloniidae)	5	Hawksbill turtle
		Snapping turtles (Chelydridae)	2	Alligator snapper
		Freshwater turtles (Emydidae)	76	Diamondback terrapin
		Tortoises (Testudinidae)	40	Giant tortoise
		Softshell turtles (Trionychidae)	20	Florida soft-shell turtle
	Side-necked turtles (Pleurodira)	Snake-necks (Chelidae)	21	Matamata
		Side-necks (Pelomedusidae)	14	Twist-necked turtle

Skin and Bone

Reptiles live all over the world except in cold deserts. Many live successfully in hot desert conditions. Their skin is an important key to survival in such extreme conditions.

Reptile skin is dry and covered in **scales**. Scales are thick pieces of dead skin. Not all scales are the same. Scales can be as tough as the strong crest on a crocodile's back but as delicate as the smooth scales of a corn snake.

Out with the old

Lizards and snakes shed their skin regularly when it gets old or worn. This is called molting. The skin of tortoises and crocodiles just gets thicker with larger scales as they grow.

Dry and warm

All scaly skin is tough enough to help protect the reptile's soft insides. It is also waterproof. This helps the reptile's body prevent water loss through **evaporation,** allowing them to live in dry places.

Scaly skin may keep water in, but it loses heat easily. Because they are **cold-blooded,** reptiles need to **bask** to get enough energy to move. Crocodiles bask on warm riverbanks, some lizards stand with their sides facing the sun, and snakes may coil up on the warm earth. As with other animals, too much heat can damage a reptile's body. In very hot **habitats,** reptiles usually hide from the sun during the day.

Marine iguanas stand up to soak up energy from the sun after swimming in the cold sea.

Vertebrate variations

The name *reptile* comes from the Latin word *repere*, which means "crawling." Not all reptiles crawl, however. Reptiles have different-shaped skeletons because they live in many different ways.

Like all **vertebrates**, reptiles have a tough but flexible internal backbone. The backbone, which supports the body, is connected to other bones such as ribs. These bones protect **organs** such as the heart from damage. Turtles have an outer shield of horn, called a shell, that covers a dome of plate-shaped ribs, which is connected to the backbone. This forms a protective box around their bodies.

The scales on this pit viper's body are different sizes. Tough scales help protect the front of its head as it moves and catches food.

The backbone is also connected to limbs for movement. Lizards and crocodiles have four short, angled legs that carry the body just above the ground. Snakes move without legs. They have flexible backbones that are connected to as many as 400 ribs. They slither along, twisting their bodies to and fro using strong muscles.

Most reptiles have teeth. Crocodiles have a mouthful, but some snakes have just a few inside their throats. They use these for gripping food as they swallow it. Turtles have no teeth but use their jaw bones for biting. Reptiles have no chewing teeth, so they swallow food whole or rip off chunks.

Reptile Reproduction

Reptiles **reproduce** on land by laying eggs. Becoming dried out is one of the biggest dangers for all young animals developing inside eggs on land. To prevent this, all reptile eggs have a tiny puddle of fluid inside them.

Reptile eggs

Reptile eggs come in different shapes and sizes. Some are shaped like big jelly beans, others like ping-pong balls or even knobbly carrots. Most reptile eggs are surrounded by a soft, leathery skin. But some, such as gecko eggs, have a hard shell like that of a bird's egg. Inside each egg is a special but delicate skin that the baby can breathe through, a bag of watery fluid, and a yolk for nourishing the developing reptile. Reptile eggs are more delicate than birds' eggs. If you turn a turtle egg over, for example, the baby turtle inside will probably suffocate and die because the special skin can be easily damaged.

Sea turtles return to the same warm beaches each year to lay their eggs. They dig holes with their legs and lay hundreds of eggs deep in the sand.

Incubation and hatching

Reptile babies can develop and hatch only if their eggs stay at the right temperature. This is called **incubation.** Parent reptiles have different ways of making sure the eggs are warm enough. Alligators living by cool, shady riverbanks lay their eggs in mounds of leaves, which produce warmth as they rot. Pythons coil around their eggs and shiver their muscles to keep them warm.

Covering eggs to incubate them also hides them from **predators,** such as egg-eating birds. Most female reptiles abandon their eggs once they are laid, but some, such as alligators, guard their eggs until they hatch. When reptiles hatch they look like tiny versions of their parents. Most of them can take care of themselves right away.

Internal incubation

Some **species** of reptiles, such as pit vipers, incubate and hatch their eggs inside their bodies. Although this means the eggs have more protection, it also means these reptiles have fewer eggs. After all, there is not much room inside!

Young alligators, like many other reptiles, have a special egg tooth on their upper jaw. They use this tooth to cut their way out of the tough shell when they hatch.

Skinks, Geckos, and Other Lizards

Lizards (**order** Squamata) are the largest group of reptiles. They have distinct necks and tails, ear openings behind their eyes, and usually four legs. Although many lizards look like crocodiles on the outside, they are similar to snakes on the inside. For example, like snakes, lizards have sensitive pits in their mouths called Jacobson's organ, which they use for taste. Lizards are therefore classified in the same order as snakes. Lizards, however, have fewer bones in their skulls than snakes do.

The largest family

The skink **family** (Scincidae) contains the largest number of **species** of all lizard families. Skinks are usually 6 to 8 inches (15 to 30 centimeters) long and live everywhere in the world, usually on the ground or hidden in burrows. They are grouped together because they have no obvious neck and they have smooth skin covered with shiny rounded **scales**, broad tongues, scaly eyelids, and very small legs.

Sand skinks live in hot desert **habitats.** They "swim" just below the surface of the sand by wriggling their bodies from side to side. This is an easier way of getting around on shifting ground than walking on legs and toes.

*The tails of many lizards break off easily so they can escape the grip of a **predator.** A new tail then grows. This skink has a blue tail to make sure predators go for its tail rather than its delicate head.*

Sticking around

Geckos (family Gekkonidae) are small climbing lizards that live in warm parts of the world. They are grouped together because they have toes **adapted** for climbing and no scales on their heads. Many geckos have no eyelids. They clean their eyes by licking them.

Geckos are mainly **nocturnal** and catch and eat insects. They are very noisy, usually making repeated calls to let other geckos know where they are. When they are frightened, the screech of baby leopard geckos sounds like air leaving the stretched end of a balloon.

Legless lizards

Several lizard families have no legs. This is an adaptation that helps them move through the thick grass and loose earth they live in. Despite their name, slow-worms (family Anguidae) are lizards, not worms. They have scaly bodies, hard skulls, and eyes with lids.

All alone

The tuatara lives on islands off New Zealand. It looks like a lizard but is classified in a group all its own. This is partly because of the number of holes in its skull and the position of its teeth.

Gecko toes have ridged, bristle-covered pads and sharp claws, which make it easy for geckos to climb, even on smooth surfaces such as glass.

Slow-worms are most active at dusk. They hunt slow-moving prey such as slugs and worms.

Iguana and Monitor Groups

The iguana group includes iguanas, agamids, and chameleons. They are all lizards with heavy bodies, short necks, fleshy tongues, and numerous belly **scales**. The other major group of lizards is the monitor group, which includes monitor lizards and beaded lizards. They have tiny, knobbly scales on their backs and forked tongues.

Iguanas and agamids

Iguanas (**family** Iguanidae) are generally large lizards that live on land, in trees, and even in the sea in North, Central, and South America. Many male iguanas have crests and brightly colored throat fans that they display to attract females or to warn other males to stay away. Rhinoceros iguanas have thick scales, which look like horns on their heads, and a heavy build to avoid being damaged in fights.

This frilled dragon is warning other animals to get away. It does this by spreading its frill, hissing, and moving forward.

Agamids (family Agamidae) live in different parts of the world than iguanas do. One **species,** called the frilled dragon, runs away fast on its back legs when it sees a possible **predator.** If cornered, the frilled dragon stretches open a frill of skin around its neck using special **cartilage** struts by its throat. The moloch, or "thorny devil," is covered with thornlike scales to repel predators. If frightened, it tucks in its head to become a prickly ball.

Hidden hunters

Chameleons (family Chamaeleontidae) look very different from iguanas and agamids. They are specially **adapted** for life in trees hunting for insects. They have a long sticky tongue, eyes that can swivel in different directions, a gripping tail, and long legs with joined toes shaped like tongs. They use their toes to grip branches. Chameleons also have **camouflaged** skin. Not only does a chameleon's skin change color for defense, it also changes with the reptile's mood. An angry chameleon can turn black with rage.

A chameleon swivels its eyes in different directions to watch out for insect prey. When it spots a meal, it moves in closer and catapults its tongue to catch it.

The monitor group

Monitor lizards (family Varanidae) have long heads and sharp claws and can swim well. They can be massive. The Komodo dragon, for example, can grow to ten feet (three meters) long. It hides in the dense forest on certain Indonesian islands. There it waits to ambush its prey, such as wild boar.

The gila monster and the beaded lizard (family Helodermatidae) live in hot deserts and are the only two poisonous lizards. Their backs have striking patterns of black, pink, or yellow scales. These markings warn other animals to keep away. If attacked, they will bite and a strong poison will run along grooves in their teeth and into their victim.

Snakes are classified in the same **order** (Squamata) as lizards because they have similar skeletons. They are grouped in a different suborder (Serpentes) from lizards because all snakes are different from lizards in several ways.

What are snakes?

Snakes have long bodies, short tails, and no legs. They have no ear openings. Instead of hearing, they sense movements around them, feeling vibrations through the ground. Instead of moveable eyelids, they have transparent **scales** to protect their eyes. All snakes are **carnivores.** Their jaws are flexible and loosely connected to their skull so they can open their mouths wide, even dislocating or unhinging their lower jaws to eat large **prey.**

Snakes can be divided into those that inject **venom** into their prey and those that do not. Rear-fangs, pythons, and burrowers do not inject venom.

The king snake is a rear-fang snake that eats prey ranging from frogs to rattlesnakes.

Rear-fangs

Rear-fangs are the largest snake **family** (Colubridae). They live around the world and include king snakes, corn snakes, and garter snakes. Their name comes from the large teeth at the back of their jaws that most use to grip their prey as they swallow. Some rear-fangs use their fangs to slit open eggs they have eaten, so they can swallow the contents. A few rear-fangs produce weakly venomous saliva but they cannot inject it.

In the loop

Boas and pythons (family Boidae) include the largest snakes, such as the anaconda of South America and the reticulated python of Asia. The anaconda can grow up to 33 feet (10 meters) long. These snakes are grouped together because they have large belly scales, obvious necks, and flexible upper jaws. Most live in trees, gripping branches with their belly scales. Some, like the anaconda, live mostly in water.

Boas and pythons kill large prey—usually **mammals** ranging from rats to deer—by squeezing them to death. This is called constriction. They bite and crush smaller prey in their jaws.

Burrowers

Some families of snakes are grouped together because they are **adapted** for burrowing. Blind snakes (family Typhlopidae) have thin, wormlike bodies. They use their hard, blunt heads to push through soil, getting a grip with the sharp spine on their tails. They have tiny eyes, as they live in dark burrows. And they find their prey, mainly ants, using their sense of smell. Their scales protect them from ant bites, but some also produce bad smells that repel ants.

Constrictors catch their prey with their sharp teeth and then coil their bodies around it to suffocate it.

Venomous Snakes

Cobras, vipers, and sea snakes inject **venom** to **paralyze** or kill their **prey.** They may also threaten to use venom as a defense if a **predator** tries to attack them. When a snake is close enough to its prey, it strikes by jabbing its fangs into the target and injecting venom. It then pulls its fangs away quickly, because they are fragile and can easily be damaged. Only when the poison has worked will the snake swallow its prey. Venomous snakes are classified by the type of teeth they have.

Fixed fangs

The cobra group (**family** Elapidae) includes snakes such as the king cobra, krait, taipan, and mamba. They are grouped together because their fangs are fixed in position in their upper jaw. Fixed-fang snakes are mostly **nocturnal** hunters. Once they have bitten their prey, their venom moves down grooves in their fangs and into the victim. Fixed-fang snakes mostly feed on rats, lizards, and frogs.

Rattlesnakes are pit vipers that get their name because they have loosely connected segments at the tip of their tails. The snake shakes its tail in defense, making a noise to ward off other creatures. For attack, it has long folding fangs.

Folding fangs

Snakes in the family Viperidae, the vipers, are classified together because their long, curved fangs are hollow, connected to venom **glands,** and fold into their mouths. When vipers strike, they fold their fangs down, and large muscles at the back of their diamond-shaped heads pump venom through the fangs and into their victim. When not in use, their fangs fold up into grooves in their mouths for protection.

Vipers usually **ambush** their prey. Pit vipers have special pits on their heads that they use to detect heat given off by approaching **mammals** such as mice. Young copperheads hide in fallen leaves and wiggle their yellow tail tip so it resembles a worm. They do this to attract worm-eating prey such as frogs.

Sea snakes

One group of snakes is **adapted** for life in shallow **tropical** seawater. Members of the family Hydrophiidae have flat tails for swimming. They come to the surface to breathe air into their lungs, close valves over their nostrils, and dive for up to five hours. Sea snake venom is generally stronger than other snake venom, so they can paralyze their slippery fish prey quickly before it gets away.

A deadly mixture

Venom is special spit made in large venom glands in the snake's head. It contains a mixture of chemicals. Some of these chemicals paralyze or kill the prey, but others help the snake to **digest** the prey.

Sea snakes hunt for fish prey such as eels in holes in coral reefs.

Turtles in Freshwater Habitats

Turtles are among the easiest to recognize of all reptiles. All turtles (**order** Chelonia) have short bodies covered by a rigid, box-shaped **carapace.** The carapace is a layer of hard, large **scales** that covers flat, arched rib bones, which are attached to the backbone. Many turtles also have a tough shell under their bellies called a plastron.

Turtles have no teeth, although many can bite well. Their jaws are often beaklike and have sharp edges. Most turtles live in shallow freshwater and can hold their breath underwater. Their legs are **adapted** for swimming, as they have either a broad, flat shape—similar to flippers—or webbed toes.

Pond turtles

Freshwater turtles (**family** Emydidae) make up about one-third of all turtle **species,** such as terrapins and painted, bog, and wood turtles. They live in pond, marsh, or **estuary habitats** of Asia and North and South America. All freshwater turtles have hard, domed shells and eat insects, snails, and fish. If attacked by a **predator,** box turtles pull in their heads, legs, and tails and raise their plastron to meet their carapace to form a tight protective box.

Freshwater turtles, such as this red-eared terrapin, have stout legs with webbed toes for life both on land and in water.

Fearsome turtles

Snapping turtles (family Chelydridae) have very sharp jaws and thick, ridged shells, which are often covered with growing pondweed. The alligator snapper of the southern United States can weigh 200 pounds (90 kilograms). It has a muscular, wormlike growth on its tongue that it wiggles to lure inquisitive prey such as fish, frogs, or other turtles. Snapping turtles also eat water plants and floating fruit.

A softer side

Softshell turtles (family Trionychidae) have flat, smooth carapaces covered with leathery skin instead of scales. They live in rivers, streams, and wetlands. Soft shells provide less protection than hard shells, but they are lighter to carry around. Many softshell turtles, such as the Chinese softshell, have long necks and noses that they use like snorkels to breathe while remaining mostly hidden underwater.

Side-necked turtles

Most turtles pull their necks straight back under their carapaces for protection. They are classified together in the suborder Cryptodira. Side-neck turtles such as the matamata are classified in a separate suborder, Pleurodira, because they pull in their necks by folding them sideways.

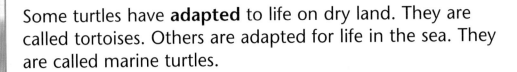

Turtles on Land and in the Sea

Some turtles have **adapted** to life on dry land. They are called tortoises. Others are adapted for life in the sea. They are called marine turtles.

Tortoises

Tortoises (**family** Testudinidae) have stubby heads and high, dome-shaped **carapaces** covered with large **scales.** Their feet are shaped like clubs for walking and have long, heavy claws for digging in hard ground.

Most tortoises are **herbivores.** Garden tortoises avoid cold seasons by burrowing into leaves and **hibernating.** Desert tortoises dig burrows up to 40 feet (12 meters) long, which they use to shelter themselves from the heat. Giant tortoises live on various islands. The Galapagos Islands in the Pacific Ocean were named after the Spanish word for the giant tortoises, *galapago,* found there. Giant tortoises may reach lengths of more than 3 feet (1 meter), weigh more than 500 pounds (225 kilograms), and live to be 100 years old. They like to cool down in muddy ponds when it is hot.

Some Galapagos giant tortoises such as this one are called saddlebacks because their carapaces arch like saddles. This allows them to stretch their necks to eat taller plants.

*This marine turtle's carapace and **plastron** are streamlined. Their smooth shape helps it move easily through the water, slowly flapping its front flippers.*

Marine turtles

Two families of large turtles live almost their whole lives at sea. Most marine turtles, such as the green turtle or olive ridley sea turtle, have hard, smooth carapaces and are classified in the family Cheloniidae. The leatherback turtle is classified separately, because its ridged carapace is covered with **cartilage** instead of scales. This makes it more like leathery skin. It can reach nearly 10 feet (3 meters) in length and weigh more than 1,100 pounds (500 kilograms). It swims over large areas of open ocean, feeding on slow-moving **prey** such as jellyfish, which it grips with its jagged beaklike jaws and the spines inside its throat.

Marine turtles often **migrate** very long distances to lay their eggs on land. The female green sea turtle may live 30 years before she is ready to lay eggs. She then migrates up to 1,240 miles (2,000 kilometers) to the same beach where she hatched, finding her way by sensing magnetic forces in the earth. It's sort of like she has a built-in compass. She then drags herself onto the beach, digs a hole with her back legs, and lays more than 200 eggs. Just a few babies will survive to grow up and return to the same beach to lay their own eggs.

True Crocodiles and Gharials

Crocodiles are massive, heavily armored reptiles grouped in the **order** Crocodilia. There are 23 **species** in the world, including true crocodiles, gharials, alligators, and caimans. Most live in **tropical** rivers and lakes.

Crocodiles use their long, muscular tails for swimming rather than their webbed hind feet. This crocodile is sliding into the water after basking in the sun.

All species of crocodiles have long bodies, heads, and tails and short legs. Their thick **scales** are strengthened with bony plates for protection. Some scales are smooth and flat, while others form hard ridges on the crocodile's back and tail. Like other reptiles, crocodiles absorb energy from the sun's warmth through their scales when they **bask** on riverbanks.

Catching food

Crocodiles usually hunt **prey** such as fish in the water, although they also catch food on land. Crocodiles have eyes and nostrils on top of their heads, so they can see and breathe while keeping their bodies and the rest of their heads hidden underwater. Their long jaws contain at least 60 heavy teeth. Crocodiles have a special flap behind their tongues to keep them from drowning when they open their mouths to catch food underwater. They produce strong stomach juices and swallow stones to help them break down food rapidly. The stones also help them stay submerged underwater.

True crocodiles

True crocodiles have long and tapering jaws. The fourth tooth from the front of the lower jaw can be seen clearly when their jaws are closed. Members of this **family** (Crocodylidae) live mostly in freshwater, but the saltwater crocodile swims in the sea between the islands where it lives. The largest, the Indopacific crocodile, can reach up to 23 feet (7 meters) in length.

Large crocodiles often catch big **mammals** or birds by surprise. Nile crocodiles wait in hiding for gnu and even lions to come for a drink at a waterhole. They then lunge out of the water, grabbing their prey and pulling it into the water to drown it. They lodge the prey between rocks or tree roots, grip on with their teeth, and then rotate their whole body to rip off bits to swallow.

Gharials

The gharial (family Gavialidae) lives in rivers in India and Nepal. It is classified separately from true crocodiles because it has very long, narrow jaws **adapted** to trap its prey—fast-moving, slippery fish. Males have a bulbous end to their snouts, which they use to make their calls louder to attract females during the **mating** season.

Gharials have many curved, sharp interlocking teeth that they use to catch fish.

Alligators and Caimans

Alligators and caimans (**family** Alligatoridae) are classified separately from crocodiles, although they look very similar. However, their jaws are broader and shorter than a crocodile's jaws, and the upper jaw overlaps the lower jaw when their mouths are closed. Also, on each side of an alligator's lower jaw, the fourth tooth fits into a socket on the upper jaw.

Alligator breeding

Alligators are unusual among crocodiles in how they care for their babies. After a female alligator has **mated,** she builds a nest out of plants and mud on a riverbank above the water. She lays about 50 eggs in the nest and covers them carefully. She then stays on guard nearby for around two months as they **incubate.** She does this because many animals, such as monitor lizards and raccoons, like to eat her eggs.

When the babies hatch, they call out and the mother breaks open the nest. She even helps crack open some of her eggs so the babies can hatch more easily. The babies stay together in a group. The mother guards them for up to two years, until they are big enough to look after themselves.

*The female American alligator is very protective of her babies. They will often **bask** in safety on her back or head.*

The spectacled caiman gets its name from the bony ridge that connects its eyes, which looks a bit like spectacles. Females often share a nest and share the task of looking after each other's babies after the eggs hatch.

Caimans

Caimans are close relatives of alligators, but they live in different parts of the world. Caimans live in South American rivers such as the Amazon. They have short skulls, often with ridges, and bony overlapping **scales** on their bellies.

Dwarf caimans only grow about 5 feet (1.5 meters) long—shorter than any other in the Crocodilia **order.** They have short upturned snouts that they use to dig burrows for shelter during the day. They are **nocturnal** hunters of crabs in the water, and they hunt beetles and other insects on land.

Larger caimans eat mostly fish, such as piranhas and catfish, as well as frogs. They can even leap out of the water to catch waterbirds. The black caiman, which can grow up to 20 feet (6 meters) long, catches larger **prey,** such as a kind of giant rodent called a capybara.

Ancient survivors

Ancestors of today's crocodiles first lived on the earth when dinosaurs were alive. **Fossil** bones suggest that some looked like today's crocodiles, but they were bigger and others looked a bit different. One even had hooves!

Reptiles All Over

Reptiles come in a great variety of shapes and sizes and have very different ways of life. Reptiles that look as different as tortoises and rattlesnakes are easy to classify separately. They look different because they have different **adaptations** to life. For example, a tortoise's **carapace**—which makes it look like a walking box—is an adaptation it uses for protection.

Sidewinders are adapted to their desert habitat. They move sideways to keep as much of their bodies off the burning hot sand as possible.

Same solution

Just to confuse things, other reptiles classified in different **orders** can look very similar because they have similar adaptations. For example, burrowing lizards, burrowing snakes, and worm lizards are similar in that they have no limbs and strong heads for pushing and wriggling through holes in the soil, but they belong to separate orders.

Worm, lizard, or snake?

Worm lizards look like big worms. They are long and thin, live mostly in the soil, and often have rings of scales around their bodies like the rings around worms. They are actually related to both lizards and snakes. They have scales and are **vertebrates**, for example, but are classified in a group of their own because of their different skeletons.

Classifying characteristics

Other animals may share many reptile characteristics but are classified separately because they do not share them all. For example, salamanders are vertebrates, reproduce using eggs, breathe partly through their lungs, and are **cold-blooded**. But they are classified as **amphibians** instead of reptiles, because their skin is not covered in **scales** and they breathe through their skin as well as their lungs.

Many reptiles appear to be exceptions to the classification rules. Some, such as shingleback skinks and garter snakes, give birth to live babies. In fact, they reproduce using eggs. Their babies develop within a transparent egg skin inside the mother and most hatch just after they leave the mother's body.

Classification can be difficult when characteristics overlap or are difficult to spot. The most important thing about reptile classification is that it can help us learn more about the fantastic variety of reptiles around the world.

The Komodo dragon has a special characteristic—jagged teeth. They are doubly effective for both gripping prey and making sure any bitten prey that escape die from blood poisoning.

A brief history of reptiles

Reptiles are thought to have amphibian **ancestors.** The first reptiles appeared on the earth more than 300 million years ago. Unlike amphibians, reptiles laid eggs with protective shells and had a water supply inside for their developing babies. They also had thicker skins with scales, which helped them live in warmer, drier **habitats.**

Glossary

adaptation special feature that helps an organism to survive in its habitat

ambush to lie in wait to surprise prey

amphibian class of cold-blooded animals with moist skin

ancestor relative from long in the past

bask to lie in the sun to get warm

camouflage color, shape, or pattern that disguises an animal against its background

carapace hard shell

carnivore meat-eater

cartilage rubbery tissue that is softer than bone

class level of classification grouping between phylum and order. Reptiles make up a class.

cold-blooded having a body temperature that changes depending on the surrounding temperature

descendant later generation of a type of organism

digest to break down food for use by the body

estuary place where a river meets the sea

evaporation process by which liquid water changes to vapor

family level of classification grouping between order and genus

fossil remains of ancient living creatures (usually formed from bones or shells) found in rocks

genus (plural is **genera**) level of classification grouping between family and species

gland place in an animal's body that secretes special fluids

habitat place where organisms live

herbivore plant-eater

hibernate to sleep through winter

incubate to keep eggs at the right temperature for the babies to develop

mammal class of warm-blooded animals with hair

mate to come together to produce babies

migrate to move from one place to another for part of the year

nocturnal active at night

order level of classification grouping between class and family

organ part of the body with a specific function

paralyze to stop movement

phylum (plural is **phyla**) level of classification grouping between kingdom and class

predator animal that hunts and eats other animals

prey animal that is hunted and eaten by another animal

reproduce to have babies

scales overlapping pieces that form a protective layer over reptile skin

species lowest level of classification grouping. Only members of the same species can reproduce together.

tropical living in parts of the world near the equator

venom poison

vertebrate animal with internal skeleton of bone or cartilage

More Books to Read

Green, Jen. *Reptiles.* Austin, Tex.: Raintree Publishers, 2002.

Matero, Robert. *Reptiles.* Vero Beach, Fla.: Rourke Publishing, 2001.

Parker, Steve. *Adaptation.* Chicago: Heinemann Library, 2000.

Wallace, Holly. *Classification.* Chicago: Heinemann Library, 2000.

Index